The Recruiter's Secret

Market Yourself to Employers Like a Pro

John P. Kaufman

WWW.THERECRUITERSSECRET.COM

To download our resume guide, Social Media Survival Guide, Video resources and get personal help from the author... visit www.TheRecruitersSecret.com

THE RECRUITER'S SECRET

I would like to dedicate this book to my daughters Brooke and Meadow who have shown me the true meaning of life.

Foreword

All of us at some time in our lives are faced with the daunting task of changing jobs. Sometimes it is due to choice, and sometimes necessity. However we are never taught how to aggressively market ourselves in school. We've been taught to write a resume, and include a cover letter. Then find job ads in the paper and online and apply to as many as we can and then cross our fingers and hope that a job comes our way.

In times of higher unemployment and a tighter job market it is even more important to be sure that you are marketing yourself effectively and not just following the old tired ways of finding a job. Every job a company advertises is generating hundreds of applicants all desperate to find a job.

In this book I will show you the closely held secrets used by professional Recruiters and Headhunters to market valuable people like you to companies that need them. I have included techniques to make you stand out from the crowd, and become the only job seeker considered for the job. That's right you will no longer be competing with hundreds of other applicants, you will be evaluated on your own. You will learn how to present yourself to companies in a way that simply cannot be ignored.

If you have always dreamed of what your life would be like working for a company that recognized and appreciated your potential and treats you like the STAR that you are, get ready because your entire notion of how to search for a job is about to be turned on its head. You are about to become your own recruiter, and you are about to be in demand.

Contents

1

THE PROBLEM

Most of us are faced with one of two situations at some point in our careers.

We lose our job, suddenly finding ourselves unemployed. We don't know how long we will be able to pay our bills, don't know if we'll lose our house, our car, and we don't know how much unemployment will pay and for how long. It's an unsettling feeling, and the worst part is, that most of us have done little or nothing to prepare for this day. This situation is damaging because every day you are out of work you are losing money, and your bills don't stop.

The second situation that you may have encountered is when you realize that you have become underemployed or hit a ceiling in our current employer. Underemployment is the situation you face when you are working for less than you are worth. I know that we all think we are worth millions of dollars to our employer, but that's not exactly what I'm talking about here. Every job has a market value, an average salary for someone in a similar position to yours in a similar industry in your location. Knowing your market value is an extremely important. Every dollar per hour that you are not paid today, results in thousands of dollars lost over the course of your career.

When we face either situation you will normally follow the same path that everyone else does, the path that you've been taught is the "Right Way", or the "Safe Way". You'll probably Ride out your unemployment, so that you can take a longer time to find the best job possible, (and possibly slip a much needed vacation in there as well). The problem here is that you are now living on a reduced income with a finite length. That's right, unemployment will give you less money than you are used to, and it doesn't last forever. So it's a band-aid not a solution. The second thing you'll probably do is buy the Sunday paper, and apply to every job ad you find that you think you match at least 51%. Then you'll go to the holy grail of the job-hunter: "The Internet" and search sites like Monster, CareerBuilder, and Yes, even Craigslist. If you are really ambitious you will probably package your resume up in a handy Word Document and e-mail it to every recruiter and temp agency you can find, possibly even paying a service to "Blast" your resume to thousands of recruiter's who are undoubtedly sitting by their computers waiting to be blessed with the work of art that is your resume.

What is wrong with that approach? Everybody does it right? It's what we've all been taught in school, by our parents, and even by the recruiting industry itself. It has to be the right way; it HAS TO WORK because you need a new job NOW. Following that path establishes you as someone who is most likely unemployed, and most likely desperate. You are establishing yourself as a beggar, not a chooser. When you do eventually land your next job, you will probably be sadly surprised by the offer you get, and it's not uncommon to actually have lower offers because employers feel like you need them more than they need you.

The Problem

Additionally when you sign follow the traditional approach you are doing exactly the same thing that everyone else is already doing, and aren't showing yourself, your personality, your potential. I think that we can all agree that your resume shows only a small fraction of your true value as an employee, your value as a person, and your potential contribution to your next employer. The challenge is that when you follow the traditional approach, to the person hiring you, you are nothing but your resume. And here's the really bad news, there are probably a hundred other resume's sitting on the employer's desk, or hard drive that are almost exactly like yours. Similar degree, similar job titles, similar job skills, and similar format. This significantly reduces your chance to be the one that is hired.

2

A LESSON FROM THE WILD

Admit it; you've watched those cheesy nature shows where they always show the pack of zebras cautiously approaching the local watering hole well aware of the danger that lurks beneath. Then suddenly WHAP one of the zebras is caught by a crocodile while the rest of the herd gets a quick drink, and runs to safety. The lesson here is that the Zebra's only defense to being eaten is the fact that they have large numbers and they all look the same. Their goal is to get to the watering hole without being eaten alive.

If a zebra goes to the watering hole all by himself, he is almost certainly going to get snapped up by the local Croc, but if he hides himself in the pack, he has drastically improved his chance of not being selected. Do you see how this relates to your career search yet? We simply have to reverse the goal.

Instead of the goal being to NOT be chosen, we want to figure out what give you the best chance of actually being chosen (Hired). The thing to remember is that most of the time when you apply to a job there are anywhere between ten to over a hundred other qualified applicants who have also submitted a resume.

Just like the Zebra you have large numbers, and a low chance of being selected. The trick I'll teach you throughout this program is how to become like that lonely zebra that has an almost certain chance of being selected. How to become the only applicant seriously considered for the job.

3

THERE IS A BETTER WAY

During the rest of this program I'll show you a better way to search for your next employer and set yourself up for a rewarding career at a company that you choose, not just the one that chose you. **The Recruiter's Secret** is a proven system that professional recruiters and highly successful jobseekers have used for generations to uncover exciting career opportunities for quality individuals like you. The good news is that it's much easier than you think to separate yourself from the pack and stand out as an individual and shine as a STAR.

THE REAL COST OF UNEMPLOYMENT AND UNDEREMPLOYMENT

If you find yourself unemployed, it's important to understand what this period is actually costing you. Only then will you take your job search seriously enough to affect real positive change in your life. Taking a passive approach to your job search will cost you THOUSANDS of dollars. Not fake dollars, not an accounting trick, but real money that you and your family will NEVER see again.

What is the real cost of being unemployed?

If you make $50K the cost of being unemployed is $1,407 per week. That figure is calculated by taking your annual wages of $50K Adding to it the cost of health care which will now be funded out of your savings through COBRA (That's if you can even afford health insurance during your job search). It also assumes that your employer makes a small 5% contribution to your 401K, and you have a nominal 10% growth rate on that money. This doesn't include growth on the contributions you make, only the employer side. It also doesn't include things like pensions, company cars, vacation or sick time, or any other perks. Just the concrete dollars that it cost you and your family every week you are out of work. The following chart shows you your weekly loss calculated at various income levels.

Your Direct Weekly Cost of Being Unemployed is.
If you make:
- ❖ $25,000 – Over $643 / Week
- ❖ $35,000 – Over $845 / Week
- ❖ $50,000 – Over $1,148 / Week
- ❖ $75,000 – Over $1,652 / Week
- ❖ $100,000 – Over $2,157 / Week

As you can see the cost of remaining unemployed is higher than you probably even realized. I'm not showing you these numbers to disappoint or discourage you, I am showing you this so that you understand that finding your next job should be your full time job while you are unemployed. Even if you are getting enough money from unemployment to survive, you are still missing out on a LOT of money that you will never see again.

Underemployment costs you more than you know

On the flip side, if you currently have a job, but you aren't being paid quite what you are worth, here is a number to chew on.

- ❖ For every $5,000 you are underpaid, you lose over $178,000 in gross earnings alone (Assumes nominal 5% increase pr yr, over 20 yr total, does not include gains derived from 401K or other investments)

So if you are stuck in a job making $30,000 a year, and the market value for your position is $35,000 a year, then it is costing you $178,000 to stay in your current job. If you are working at a position for $60K and you should be making $70K it is costing you $356,000.00 to stay in your current job. If you are currently making $80,000 and you are worth $100,000 it will cost you $712,000 to stay in your current job.

I see what's happening , you're yelling at me right now saying: " John you are dead wrong. If I make $5 Thousand, or $10 Thousand too little, it cost me exactly that, less after taxes. It's really not that big of a deal, and after all, I'm comfortable in my job. The people are nice, they treat me well,,,, I even got a ham last holiday, or wait, was that two holidays ago… anyways you must be wrong, because If I was losing THAT MUCH money I'd surely have realized it before."

Please re-read the section and understand that I'm not saying that you will lose $178,000 a year For every $5,000 in underpayment, but $178,000 over the next 20 years. This includes the fact that if you get a raise each year it's probably based on what you make now. So if you get a 5% raise on a $30,000 salary, it's significantly less of a raise than you will get if you make $35,000. If you are ever recruited to change jobs, your new salary will probably be based on a percentage increase (usually between 5-10%) of your current salary. So remaining in a job where you are underpaid will even reduce the amount you will make on your next job. So you can figure it out yourself exactly how it applies to you, but understand that the amount of money you are losing if you are underemployed is HUGE, and the longer you wait to fix this the less money you will have over the course of your career. Every promotion you have been passed over for, every year you go without a raise, or simply are too lazy to find out what your true value actually is, is a year wasted, is a year that you permanently lower your earning power for the rest of your life. The only way to fix this problem is to STOP WAITING and start EARNING.

OK, Now that I've finally convinced you to take the plunge and explore the job market, what's your next move? Well, you could follow the traditional job seeker approach.

The traditional job-seeker approach

❖   Has a feeling that cutbacks are coming, sees signs

- ❖ Loses Job
- ❖ Takes some time to relax before getting back in the market
- ❖ Starts asking friends if they know of any available jobs
- ❖ Starts clipping ads from paper
- ❖ Applies to online jobs at job boards like monster or Career-Builder
- ❖ Gets 1 callback for every 100-150 jobs that he applies to
- ❖ Gets frustrated
- ❖ Starts contacting Recruiters and Employment agencies
- ❖ Unemployment runs out
- ❖ Takes a lower paying job than his previous one, or out of his field (If Unemployed - formerly in corporate management, now working in retail to survive)
- ❖ May take years to get back to his previous salary if ever (If Unemployed)

Admit it; you've done exactly this the last time you were looking for a job. Hopefully it turned out well for you, but many times it doesn't. Following the traditional approach makes for a long and painful job search for many people. Most start out pretty strong with lots of enthusiasm, and put in a bit of work in the beginning, but once the frustration starts setting in the hours spent looking for a job tail off, and in the end most people end up taking a job that is out of their field, or below their skill level just to be able to pay some of the bills and survive. The thing you need to understand is that IT DOES NOT NEED TO TAKE 6 MONTHS to GET A NEW JOB. If you focus early on, and begin the search in the right way you'll be back to work much   more   quickly.

5

RECRUITERS AND EMPLOYMENT AGENCIES

What about recruiters and employment agencies, don't they find us jobs for a living? The short answer here is NO. I know that when you are approached by a recruiter or talk to an employment (Temp Staffing) agency they might tell you that their only concern is finding you a job, and that they want to help you. This is probably true, because we are all human, we are generally compassionate, and are in this business because we want to help people. The sad truth however is that recruiters and temp agencies don't make money by finding you a job, they make money by finding people for companies. What's the difference? Recruiters and Agencies are paid by employers to find **specific people** that the **company** WANTS to hire. This means that a recruiter or agency can be helpful as long as you fit the profile of the specific person that one of their clients wants to hire, but if you don't you'll probably be left with little to show for all of the recruiter's or agency's good intentions.

It's important to understand the difference between a Recruiter and an Employment (Temp staffing) Agency.

Recruiters

- ❖ Recruiters find candidates for perm placement at companies within their niche. They usually specialize in a specific field like accounting, IT Management, Web Developers, HR professionals, Sr. Management, Engineers, Medical, etc... They are actively looking for people that work within their niche to present to employers within it.
- ❖ Are paid a large fee by the hiring company for bringing them a candidate that they couldn't find on their own. This means someone who's resume isn't on the job boards, hasn't already applied at that company, and isn't actively looking for a job.
- ❖ Often talk about a "Hidden Job Market" - A pool of jobs known only to recruiters, and not available to the general public. (The hidden market is really opportunities created for star quality candidates where companies didn't previously recognize a need for a particular candidate)
- ❖ Will actively market exceptional candidates within their niche
- ❖ Will attempt to match "inventory" candidates to open job orders

Employment Agency (AKA Temp Agency, or Staffing Agency)

❖ Employment Agencies – tend to work with more generalized markets IE Clerical, or office help, General Labor, etc…

❖ Tend to work locally – Usually are operating within a small geographic area, county, or city.

❖ Place candidates in largely clerical or unskilled positions

❖ Place candidates in short term or temp-hire positions

❖ Work with average candidates to just get them any job, not to get them the best job available.

❖ Are paid a % of the hourly wages of a large number of candidates that are all in the field working at any given time.

❖ Work primarily with "Inventory Candidates"

6

AREE YOU A "MARKETING CANDIDATE" OR AN "INVENTORY CANDIDATE"?

The first thing that I want to mention here is that the above are industry insider terms, and are not meant to judge the qualifications, or quality of any particular person. So please don't be offended if you end up in a category that you didn't want. The terms are used to quickly identify the prospects of a **particular candidate** being actively marketed by a **particular recruiter**. So if you are a marketing candidate to one recruiter, you may very well be an inventory candidate to another.

Because Recruiters tend to work within a certain niche (area of specialization) he will generally be interested in candidates whom are actively employed and meet certain requirements within his niche. As a general rule though you can do a simple self assessment to determine if you might be a marketable candidate within your own job niche.

17

A marketing candidate is typically someone who has a **unique** characteristic derived through education, experience and accomplishment, and has this skill or expertise in a field that is currently in demand.

Characteristics of a Marketable Candidate

- ❖ Education
    - o Engineering
    - o Nursing
    - o Legal
    - o IT
- ❖ Special Skills or Experience
    - o Sales
    - o Project Management
    - o Programming
    - o Executive Experience
- ❖ Works in a field with a labor shortage
    - o Engineers
    - o Medical Workers
    - o Skilled Trades (Electricians, etc…)
- ❖ Is currently employed
    - o Has been with current employer for a sustained time,
    - o Doesn't often change jobs
- ❖ Is NOT Actively looking for a job
    - o Is not applying for jobs
    - o Doesn't have his resume posted online
    - o Hasn't contacted every recruiter on the internet

Recruiters are paid for bringing a candidate to a company that they **couldn't have otherwise found** by themselves. This means that **if you are available for free, a recruiter can't get paid** for marketing you to his clients. This is often called being in competition with your recruiter and will immediately get you taken off the marketable candidate list, and put into the inventory candidate list. So prior to contacting recruiters be sure that you are NOT actively looking, and are willing to allow him time to do marketing on your behalf.

Characteristics of an Inventory Candidate

Inventory Candidates are:

Candidates that are qualified for positions within their industries but may have any of the following characteristics

May lack star quality – Not enough experience, or Accomplishments. Or average resume compared to other candidates within your field.

Are actively seeking employment – You may be a STAR in your field, but if you are applying to every company in your field, blasting resume's to recruiters, and have a resume posted on every job related website, you'll be labeled an inventory candidate

Have frequent job changes – If you have a new job every year or two you will not be marketable because companies want to hire long term employees.

Unemployed – if you are unemployed, the same recruiters that once beat down your door now treat you like you have the plague.

Inventory candidates will generally not be marketed, but put into a recruiter's database

Generally there are tens of thousands of "Inventory Candidates" in a typical recruiter's database

They are contacted only in the event that a job comes along that would be such a good fit for that candidate that he is a shoe-in, or if there are no marketable candidates available for a particular position.

Contacted again in a few years in the hopes that he landed on his feet and is now a marketable candidate again.

You can see the difference in how a recruiter will treat you if you are a marketing candidate vs. an inventory candidate. It's not because recruiters are evil or because companies are evil but due to the economic realities of business. The first thing to realize is that people place a higher value on that which they cannot have. It's basically the only reason that a Mercedes is worth more than a Chevrolet. Both cars perform the exact same function (Drive from point A to point B), and do it in the same way. They can both be adorned with leather, and shiny chrome wheels. The main difference that gives a Mercedes its prestige is its scarcity. You can buy a Chevy, Honda or Ford at almost every new and used car dealer in America, find one for sale on every street, and park next to one on a daily basis without even trying. These "average cars" are so common that they become all but invisible to someone that wants the prestige of a Mercedes. A Mercedes (Or Porsche, BMW, Audi, Cadillac, Hummer, etc…) on the other hand is rare. If you want to find just the Mercedes you are looking for, you might have to buy one from half way across the country and have it shipped in. You probably won't park next to another one just like it at the grocery store very often either.

The point I'm trying to make here is that, to a recruiter, when you are easily available your value goes down. When you are in demand, yet unavailable, recruiters will place a high value on you.

How does this change your likelihood of getting a job through a recruiter?

Marketing candidates typically get multiple interviews in a couple of weeks, and have serious offers almost immediately. They also tend to get increases in pay and benefits over their previous position due to the recruiter's active marketing and positioning the candidate as a STAR.

Inventory Candidates are a recruiter's last resort. They may never get an interview generated by a recruiter, or may get an interview months or years later. Have a flatter earnings curve over the course of their career due to less opportunities being presented.

As you can see, if you plan on working with a recruiter you had better find a way to position yourself as a marketing candidate.

WORKING WITH A RECRUITER

You may have been approached by a recruiter at some point in your career when you were identified as a potential "Marketing Candidate" Or you may have contacted a recruiter when you decided that you would like to explore the job market, or were unemployed. So I don't have to tell you that recruiters are strange. When you don't want a job, they won't leave you alone, and when you need a job they don't have time to say hello. Now that you have read the section about Marketing Candidates vs. Inventory Candidates you should understand why that happens a little better.

Working with a recruiter is an excellent option when looking for a job because recruiters market candidates for a living, and know how to do it effectively. A recruiter can act as your "Agent" and help you negotiate a higher salary, benefits, and relocation packages. We work with you to ease the transition because we do this stuff for a living, and we have seen it all.

I do think it's important to go over what you should expect when working with a recruiter. I you are approached by a recruiter that is interested in marketing you, the recruiter will generally approach you with some job offer that may or may not be a great fit for you. During the conversation he becomes interested in your potential as a marketing candidate and would like you to give him some additional information. The things he needs are related to what your ideal position would be, where it would be located, how much you would want to earn, etc.… Following a brief conversation he will probably send you a document requesting some career history, salary history, and requesting references. If this happens fill it out and return it to him quickly. Not only does he need this information, but it is a test. Yes, he is testing you to see if you are actually serious about changing jobs. If you take a long time on the little "Homework" assignments he gives you, he will determine that you are not serious, not reliable, or not honest. Either way, the recruiter will probably disappear faster than you can blink your eyes. Recruiters don't always deliver the results for you that you hoped, but they generally do try hard. Their livelihoods depend on finding quality individuals and placing them in new positions. They are paid on a commission only basis, and if they determine at any time that they can't trust you, they have no choice but to move on to help someone that they can work with in an open an honest relationship.

The other thing that a quality recruiter that is serious about marketing you (vs. using you to fill an open job order) will want is an agreement that you will work exclusively with him in your job search. Again the reason is that a recruiter makes his living by presenting "Marketable" candidates to employers. And a major part of what makes a candidate marketable is the fact that he is not actively looking for a job elsewhere. If you are working with a recruiter on an exclusive basis he will want you to remove your resume from any online databases, and possibly reduce your profile on social networking sites such as LinkedIn or Facebook in order to reduce your online footprint, and make you more marketable. If he finds out that you are conducting any job search activities or distributing your resume in any way that he wasn't previously aware of, he will conclude that he can't market you and will no longer help. You will want to keep him apprised of ALL job search activity that you may be conducting on your own.

The worst case scenario – If you are working with a recruiter and you have submitted a resume either directly or through a friend prior to or subsequent to the recruiter presenting you to the employer and it is found out during the hiring process, it makes both you and the recruiter look bad. The employer assumes that a recruiter should know that you applied if he did his research, and assumes that you should have told the recruiter about this. This makes the recruiter look incompetent and you look dishonest at the same time. This gives the employer two very big reasons not to hire you. Now let's assume for a minute that the employer gets past the assumptions of dishonesty and incompetence. In the end, I've never seen a candidate get hired in this type of situation. The recruiter will then drop the candidate as a client and he will be on his own again.

The best case scenario - You are working with a recruiter who is actively marketing you. You give him a list of companies where you have previously applied or had career related contact with (within the last year). The recruiter works with you to find opportunities that fit your profile, presents you as a STAR quality candidate, negotiates an increase in salary over your previous position, and assists you in interview preparation, scheduling, and the transition to your new career. The employer is happy because the recruiter presented him with such a quality employee, you are happy because you have improved your career prospects and are a step closer to your long term goals, and the recruiter is happy because he helped someone along their career path, and fed his family.

The bottom line to working with a recruiter is to be honest, bet reliable, and communicate openly with the recruiter. Most of us really have your best interest at heart and are always open to suggestions on how to more effectively market you and to whom.

SHOULD I MARKET MYSELF?

If you don't feel that you fit the profile of what a recruiter would consider a marketable candidate, or you just can't find one to actively market you, don't be discouraged. You can always market yourself; it's what you'd be doing anyway if you were to apply to every job in town right? You just wouldn't call it marketing, you'd call it the "Traditional Jobseeker Approach", and it wouldn't be as effective as the techniques I'm about to teach you.

If you are not working with a recruiter but would like the many benefits of being actively marketed you can market yourself. Here is where the work really begins for you. I'm going to ask you to trust me, and please put in the effort. What I'm about to teach you is the real "Recruiter's Secret". Once you learn the methods and follow this plan you may be interviewing with companies that didn't even know they were hiring. You will be the lone Zebra wading in knowing that you're about to be snatched up by the employer you choose.

Part of this plan does involve minimal cost on your part, primarily for things like mailing labels, envelopes, stamps, and other office supplies. The cost to do all of this is quite low, and if you were paying attention to the actual cost of being unemployed or underemployed the total cost of following my program will be less than the cost of being unemployed for even a couple of days. If you follow this system and do a good job on it, the benefit will be finding a new good paying job at an employer of your choosing and spending several months less than you may have otherwise. You may land your first interviews in a couple of days or weeks, instead of getting one re-ply from every 100-150 applications submitted online. Additionally you'll have an opportunity to earn a higher salary because you'll be presenting yourself as a STAR and won't be directly competing with a herd of other applicants.

When Should I Market Myself?

One of the single most important factors in your marketing success is actually making the decision to market yourself. The question of when is significantly less important than simply making the decision in the first place. But you should remember that in general the sooner the better is the rule you should follow here. Waiting simply prolongs your current situation and reduces the opportunities you will have, and reduces the income you will earn.

Start marketing yourself BEFORE you have lost your job if possible.

Remember that you are the most valuable, when you are unavailable. So waiting until you lose your job to start marketing yourself will cost you significant amounts of money, and make it more difficult to land a position that it an improvement over your current one. So beware of the signs of impending layoffs and begin your marketing efforts in advance.

Be aware of the signs

- ❖ Slower sales
- ❖ Cutbacks in other departments
- ❖ Buyouts / Mergers
- ❖ Rumors

As much as we like to say we are surprised by a layoff, a merger, or company closing, or being fired deep down it's rarely a complete surprise. If we pay attention to what's going on with our employers we are rarely caught completely off guard when a change happens. Admit it, you've been caught before in the "They'll probably lay someone off but I'll be safe because ……." game. And then the layoffs come, and you might be safe the first time, or you might not. But someone that you thought was completely safe, got let go. He thought he was safe because…… too.

Be proactive

Start your plan with at least 6 weeks before you think you are in danger. That's right I said start your marketing plan at least 6 weeks before you think you'll be laid off. If you don't know it's coming, haven't heard any rumors, etc… then start today. It's easier to actually market yourself when you've done the leg work in advance. It's also much less stressful to find out that an impending layoff is on its way when you are prepared. Assuming that you do have some notice you need to remember that it is easier to market yourself when you are employed because you are unavailable (Chevy vs. Mercedes) and companies will pay extra to get you, vs. giving you a lowball offer because they think you're desperate.

The other reason that it's important to begin early is because it takes time to market yourself, get interviewed, get a job offer, make the decision and change jobs. Even if you are a start quality candidate, do a fantastic job marketing yourself, and get an offer from the first company you interview with, the process will probably take at least a couple of weeks. So in the best case scenario, if you sense an impending layoff 4 weeks out, start marketing yourself today, and get an offer within 2 weeks. That still leaves 2 weeks notice, and a total of 4 weeks to change jobs….. which coincidentally is the same amount of time you had before being laid off. You have probably just saved yourself from un uncertain amount of time on the unemployment line, saved yourself thousands of dollars, and probably got a salary increase in the process. As for your old employer, they no longer have to lay you off, and you've probably saved the job of one of your co-workers.

If you are already unemployed

Start marketing yourself ASAP – let me repeat that – Start marketing yourself ASAP!!! Remember that now you are unemployed Time is

Money, and Time is Your Enemy. Please refer to the section on the cost of unemployment to calculate how much it's costing you for every week you aren't working. The other factor you need to be aware of is that the longer you are out of work the lower your eventual offers will be if you find another job within your field. When employers see someone has been unemployed or 5, 6, 8, months, they know that you are getting desperate, and will probably accept any offer they give you. If you receive an offer within your field, it may be 10% - 20% or more under your fair value. You also might have to take a job for less than your value or out of your field just to survive. I have spoken to many downsized 6-figure executives that have had to take jobs at Wal-Mart, Best Buy or Lowes because once they were unemployed for too long their value went down and the big money offers from recruiters that they were used to for their entire careers never came. They relied on the traditional jobseeker approach, and didn't understand why for their entire careers they had been marketable candidates, and all of a sudden they were excess inventory. A proactive self marketing approach can prevent this from happening to you.

9

DETERMINE YOUR MARKET VALUE

The first thing that you need to understand when searching for a new job, or determining your market value is that unless you have changed something significant about your background, for example added a new degree which is unrelated to your current experience, your value will be greatest if you remain in your current field, and in your current industry. For example: Someone with 15 years of accounting experience in manufacturing and a B.S. in accounting and a CPA certification will be most valuable to another manufacturing company if he stays in a similar role (possibly advanced to controller or CFO depending on experience) but the unique knowledge he has gained regarding manufacturing is an asset to another manufacturing company. Things like job costing, inventory valuation, etc... are similar in all industries, but there are significant differences in the actual management of companies in manufacturing vs. services, agricultural, or non-profit organizations. Additionally any software or management systems that he has experience with will make him more valuable to a

33

similar company using similar systems. A company may pay a premium to hire this individual if it appears that he will not only fit in nicely, but will excel within their organization without any significant learning curve.

Conversely if that same accountant decided that he wanted to change careers and pursue a marketing position he would have to accept a lower role in a different company and may possibly require additional education or certifications in order to qualify. Adding an MBA in marketing would be a step in the right direction, but would not be as valuable as his current experience in accounting is if he stays within the same field.

I'm not trying to be discouraging to anyone that would like to change fields, we are not all cut out to work in a single job or type of job for our entire careers. The point that I am trying to make is that for the purposes of determining our market value it's much easier to do within a field that we have education, experience, and accomplishments in.

You are worth more if you are employed

We have already covered this to some extent in the marketing candidate vs. inventory candidate section of the program. However I would like to stress the fact that you have greater market value while you are still employed. Employers are like everyone else, they want that which they cannot have. If you have been laid off they will view you as "suspect" the thought is always there among employers that: "If you were laid off there must have been some reason". There is a common assumption within hiring circles that companies "Cull the Herd" during downsizing. That they use the excuse of cost cutting to eliminate problem, unproductive, and overpaid employees, and that they keep the best even during cutbacks. This is a completely unfair assumption, however it is an assumption that you need to overcome in order to determine your worth and properly market yourself.

A couple of resources for determining compensation available within the market.

❖ http://www.salary.com – this site will give you a reasonable idea of market value salaries for a variety of positions narrowed down by industry and location. The numbers are not 100% accurate regarding what you specifically should be making, but they are a guideline.

❖ http://www.indeed.com/salary - This is another excellent resource. They take their data from ads placed on a variety of public job boards, company websites and more. It doesn't tell you what the full compensation package is, what the actual offer that will be made and accepted by any particular employees, but again it is a general guide which is very useful.

The most accurate way to find your true market value is to simply market yourself, interview, and get an offer. The old saying that something is "only worth what someone is willing to pay for it" couldn't be truer than in the case of your market value. Each jobseeker is a unique case, and your actual value can only be determined accurately by putting yourself out there and finding out what someone is willing to pay. You might be pleasantly surprised by the offer and be better off for it, or you might find out that you already have it made. Either way the only way to find out for sure is to try.

10

IDENTIFY AND TARGET POTENTIAL EMPLOYERS

Nothing is more important to your career happiness than the company you work for. The first step in marketing yourself to potential employers is finding the companies to target. Unlike times past, there are plentiful resources available online which allow you to identify and research companies in order to effectively market yourself to them.

When researching companies to market a candidate to a recruiter takes into account factors like:

- ❖ The Company's Industry
- ❖ Company Size
- ❖ Location
- ❖ Culture

Each of these factors is important in determining a fit for you. As I mentioned previously it is generally a good idea to stay within a familiar industry. A factor that is often overlooked though is company size. The old idiom that "Size doesn't matter", definitely doesn't apply to employers. If you are comfortable working in a small family business with 10 employees where everyone knows each other, from the owner down to the newest employee, you may have a hard time adjusting to the impersonal atmosphere of a large multinational corporation with multiple layers of management and bureaucracy. The opposite is also true, and this is why as a recruiter, I try to keep people in similar size / culture companies.

As for location, it is important to understand that a company that is located too far from your home will be assuming that you won't want to commute that far, or that you might reject their offer if it was made due to the distance. If you are attempting to relocate, location is also important because you need to know that your new work environment is a reasonable distance to your new home.

Research your target companies prior to making contact

As a recruiter and a business owner I can tell you that there is nothing more annoying than receiving a generic resume in the e-mail or mail with no customization for my company, or no demonstration of any knowledge about my company, or the type of work required by the candidate. Don't make this mistake. Prior to sending out a resume / marketing package to an employer, do some research on the company. There is so much information available for free these days that there is really no excuse not to do it. And as a self marketer, this is an excellent example to prove to your employer that you are motivated, and do your homework. Bulk mailings with no personalization will get you moved to the bottom of the pile quickly.

Things you should know about your target companies: You should try to find out who their competitors are, who their customers are what their key products / services are, who their key executives are. Key executives, from the standpoint of getting yourself hired, are typically Owners, Founders, hiring Managers, line Managers would be directly supervising you if you are hired, and HR managers. I think it's also beneficial to identify and speak with anyone who is currently in a position similar to your target job. They can give you inside information on who to talk to, and how best to approach them. Knowing about their products and customers gives you something intelligent to talk about during your interview, and puts you on the inside track to getting hired. Doing research before you contact a company shows that you are motivated, intelligent, and will go the extra mile. It shows the company that you would be a valued addition because nobody else that they have ever hired has probably ever put in that kind of effort. In short, it will help you present yourself as a Star.

Your current employer's competition

It's often difficult to think of marketing yourself to your employer's competitor or customers. However in the recruiting business, we often market candidates directly to a company's competitors. They are often willing to hire someone even if there are no open jobs, just to jump at the chance to hire a key person from their competitors. Your company's customers are often willing to hire someone from a company that they respect as well. However, before you offer yourself up to the competition or customers, make sure that you don't have a non-compete agreement in effect, and that there are not any vendor / joint venture agreements between the company's not to hire each other's employees. The other pitfall to watch for is if you are conducting a confidential job search (You are still employed and don't want word to get back to your boss) then dealing with companies that have any relationship business or social with your boss could be dangerous. This is one advantage of working with a recruiter. A recruiter can market you to companies in a completely confidential manner where your name is not revealed to the hiring company until you have actually interviewed with them.

11

TOOLS FOR FINDING AND RESEARCHING COMPANIES

There are many free resources that you can use to research a company prior to contacting them. The first set of resources is Job Boards and Job Search Engines. Professional recruiters use these sites differently than the average jobseeker. Instead of using the sites to find available jobs and applying to them using the online forms, recruiters use them as information gathering tools. We learn about which companies are hiring for certain positions, and what kinds of salary's are being offered. Sometimes we find contact information for a hiring manager, or some other useful tidbit. We can also expand on this information to target a company's competitors. If Company "A" needs to hire someone like you, then Company "B" their direct competitor, might need someone like you too. The key thing to remember is that when you see the job advertised online, there will be many applicants competing for the job by submitting their resume and cover letter online. If you do the same you haven't done anything to separate yourself from the pack. I'm not saying that you shouldn't apply to

41

a company that is advertising, I'm telling you to follow my program completely and you'll separate yourself from the competition and you won't have to apply online.

Job Boards & Job Search Engines

- ❖ Monster, Careerbuilder, Hotjobs, Local Paper, Craigslist etc…
- ❖ Industry niche boards – Specific boards for computer jobs, healthcare, accounting, engineering, high salary executives, etc…
- ❖ Meta Engines like Indeed and Simply Hired – These sites search through multiple job sites at the same time as well as company career websites. They are an excellent source of information for a jobseeker.

Social networking sites are another excellent source of information about a company. Sites like LinkedIn.com often have large directories of employees of a particular company. With millions of members virtually all large companies and most small and medium companies have at least some presence on LinkedIn. Using LinkedIn is fun because you can search the name of a company and find out the names and personal profiles of people from executives all the way down to entry level staff. This will allow you to develop enough information on a lot of companies to develop a basic org chart, as well as information regarding friends you may have in common, hobbies that are shared, etc… and can give you an unfair advantage in connecting with an influential person in that company on a personal level. Sites like Facebook and MySpace are excellent resources to find additional employees, and see more personal information on them.

I'm not suggesting that you should become a stalker here, just develop a sense of the people within the company, a sense of the culture of the company, and possibly reach out to a few people that work there in order to find out information regarding what types of jobs may be available, what type of people they hire, what the culture is etc…

- ❖ Social Networking Sites
- ❖ Linkedin
- ❖ Facebook
- ❖ Myspace

Business Research Websites like Hoovers, Manta, and Zoominfo are all pretty similar. They allow you to search for companies in a particular industry, particular market size, and location. They have extensive options for narrowing or expanding your list as well, but the key thing is that they assist you in finding companies that fit your profile very quickly. They all offer some level of free searching, and if you find that you'd like more detailed information you can usually sign up for a free trial. These sites are very expensive to purchase full access to them because they are marketed to large companies' sales departments and to professional recruiters. However, there is a significant amount of information that you can learn about a company from only the free information provided. You'll be able to learn things like, who their competitors are, what their annual sales are, names of key executives, stock prices, and other information that you may find useful.

Business Research Websites

- ❖ Hoovers
- ❖ Manta
- ❖ Zoominfo
- ❖ Google Finance / Yahoo Finance

Without a doubt the most detailed information that you can get on company employees is Jigsaw.com. Jigsaw is a website that is used by the recruiting industry, as well as top producing sales professionals to quickly identify target companies, and then find out who works for them. The advantage of Jigsaw is that you can search companies in the same way that you use Hoovers, Zoominfo or Manta, but instead of detailed company information, you can get direct contact info on many of the employees at almost any company you'd like. So you can quickly get the name, phone number, and e-mail address of a Sales Manager in the Phoenix branch, of XYZ Corp, and get the same info for the HR manager in the headquarters in New York. Access to detailed information is not free, but the rates are very low considering the value of the data available. This is a tool that you simply must try. This site is a very valuable secret used daily by professional recruiters.

Most detailed business employee directory
❖ Jigsaw.com

Other sources of company information are available, and I'm not goint to go into great detail on all of them, but understand that using search engines like Google, Yahoo, etc… along with searching news items about a company can give you a lot of the information I mentioned above. Taking the time to truly research a company prior to marketing yourself to them is one of the most valuable things you can do, and will be a major factor in getting hired faster and for more money.

> ❖ Google
>> ❖ Search
>> ❖ News
>> ❖ Company Website
>> ❖ Telephone – Call into a company and ask questions about the company * a good place to start is the sales department

A note about job boards
I know that I'm repeating myself here but this is extremely important. Don't rely exclusively on job boards to find your target companies. Companies with jobs posted will be receiving multiple applications (sometimes hundreds) for the advertised positions, and applications for those positions typically have to go through HR, and

may have to be submitted electronically where they go directly into the company's "Applicant Tracking System" where your resume will be graded by keyword prior to a human even seeing it. This reduces your chance of standing out from the crowd and makes you just another applicant.

Instead use job boards to identify companies that match your target profile, and find competitors that you can market yourself to.

12

THE RECRUITER'S SECRET – RESUME GUIDE

One of the most important things you can have to get a new job is a strong resume. The fact is however, that most people make the same mistakes on their resumes and it's really no wonder. We are taught bad habits in schools, and with resume templates, etc… that are found online.

Most of the advice we have been given comes from the old days when everybody searched for a job in the local paper, and mailed physical resume's to the address or PO Box listed in the paper. Back then, it was important to keep your resume a certain length, have it printed on a certain kind of paper, have lots of action words, and follow a certain format, because it was going to be put in a physical pile, and be reviewed by a live person.

The problem with the old way of doing things is that today most resume's never get read in the first place. When you submit a resume to a job posting you have found online, chances are that it is not being read by a human, rather it is being submitted to an "Applicant Tracking System" or

ATS for short. An ATS is a software program that is designed to filter out resume's that don't fit the profile that the hiring manager is looking for. For instance, if you are applying for a job that requires you to know Microsoft Office, and Microsoft Office is not listed on your resume, your resume will be penalized. Get too low of a score, and it is disregarded, get a high score and a human will look at your resume.

The benefit of these systems to a recruiter is that they can screen thousands of resumes in a few seconds and find probable matches based on the keywords and phrases in the resume database. The problem with these systems if you are a jobseeker, is you seldom know exactly what key phrases are going to be used to search for you and that makes it less likely that your resume will even get seen.

In the marketing section of "The Recruiter's Secret" I'll cover ways that you can market yourself in order to avoid being put into the database and get your resume in front of people with the power to hire you, not the people that are hired to screen you out.

Rethinking your resume

We are taught that we should prepare a resume with a well drafted cover letter, and an objective using "Action Words" to show how great we are, and then follow that with your education and job history. However, in today's competitive job market we have to re-think that tired format.

Get rid of the objective

The first thing that I want to stress is that you should get rid of your objective. I can already hear you saying that I'm crazy, but think about it just for a minute. What is the purpose of your "Objective"? That's right, it is there to tell the reader what you want out of the relationship. We have all been told that phrases like: "Secure a position in the ABC industry where I can use my skills as an XYZ to help an employer be successful"

If you put yourself in the position of the reader, and think about what he wants, it becomes obvious that an objective is ridiculous. The person reading your resume cares about one thing and one thing only. WHAT CAN YOU DO FOR ME AND MY COMPANY – IE Will I make more money, or solve an important problem by hiring this person. Generic statements about your goals, your skills, tempered with generic references to his industry place the focus on what you want for yourself, not what you can do for the company.

A Career Summary instead of an Objective

I recommend putting a career summary where we have been taught an objective should go. A career summary is a few sentences that stress what you have already accomplished for your previous employers, and are backed up by quantitative (not subjective) facts.

IE "Lead a sales turnaround for my division, increasing sales by 100% in 6 months"
OR
"Lead a team of 6 people to increase departmental efficiency by 30%".

You'll see that these statements focus on your actions, and your value to your previous company. You are probably wondering, "What If I don't have any significant accomplishments" – We all have done something that we can put into this format. If you decreased paperclip use in your office, if you replaced two janitors by yourself and your own hard work and saved your employer money, identify it, and have it ready for your resume. It doesn't matter if you are a janitor or a manager, if you have been employed for any significant time, you have done something that can be quantified, and if you weren't creating value for your employer you would have been unemployed quickly.

What format should you use for your resume?

The complete format should be as follows:

Career Summary (Quantifiable statements related to what you have already done / what makes you valuable)

Employment history - I recommend using a reverse chronological format for your resume. This format will list your employers, most recent first, working backwards to your oldest employer.

List at least three Quantifiable Accomplishments for each employer. Quantifiable accomplishments are things you accomplished, and are backed by some concrete number. They are very similar to your career summary, other than instead of your biggest accomplishments over your career, you list several for each employer. If you have more than three that you can identify list them, but if you have too many pick the strongest ones and list them.

Unless you are in Sr. Management, I wouldn't recommend more than 5-6 for each employer. Examples of quantifiable accomplishments are: "Increased Sales by X% in Y Months", "Lead a team of X on a project lasting Y Months with a budget of $Z" or "Reduced overhead by Y% in Z Years". Including these types of facts in your resume will enable you to demonstrate that you are a quality employee, and bring value to your employer. The key is that very few people put this type of information on their resume's and if you do, you will appear to be a more valuable candidate than the others.

List at least three responsibilities for each employer - responsibilities are different than accomplishments insofar as they are things that you did on a regular basis, like maintaining spreadsheets, or checking pricing from suppliers. This is the daily duties that you performed in your job. IE "Balanced Checkbook" It's less likely that you will be able to quantify these, but if you can it's a bonus. It's important to list your responsibilities because it gives the employer a good sense of the type of work you are used to doing, and the workload you can handle. Job titles are often associated with drastically different responsibilities at different companies, so there are times when an accounting clerk at one company is performing largely the same responsibilities as a Sr. Accountant at another. The only way to break through the clutter is to make sure you have your responsibilities listed.

List all employers for at least the last 10-15 years. – It is a sad fact, but age discrimination happens every day in this country. Many employers prefer younger workers due to reduced health care costs, the perception that they'll be employed longer, and that they'll be able to handle larger workloads. It's illegal for employers to discriminate against you based on your age, however it is difficult to prove, and it does happen. If you are worried that your age will reduce your opportunities, you may want to not list every employer you had all the way back to your college days. Depending on the stage your career is in, you may wish to limit the number of employers listed to 10 years, or even 20 years if you are in a more Sr. position.

Explain any gaps in your employment – If you have any gaps in employment due to layoffs, illness etc… that last over 6 months, you may want to list a reason why you were unemployed. Long gaps in your employment history make your resume look bad. However they do happen to good people, many of us have taken time off to care for a loved one, had major health issues, etc… just be ready to explain them, and be honest. The only thing worse than giving an answer that someone doesn't like is getting caught in a lie.

Key Qualifications Section – It's important to include a key qualifications section in your resume because your work experience, accomplishments, and responsibilities may not include all of your value. If you know a software program, a programming language, have completed a

course, earned a certificate, etc… even if you don't think it's completely relevant to your job list it. However, only list things here that you actually
know well enough to be useful. Again the key here is to be honest. If I was
to list my key qualifications, I would list things like Microsoft Office, PHP,
MySQL, UNIX, etc… I am not an "Expert" at all of them, but I do know
enough about them to warrant listing them because I have hands on experience in all of them.

Education Section – It's important to list your education in your
resume. List any schools attended along with degrees earned. Also list any
qualifications earned through study courses even if they weren't provided by
a college. IE technical training for a particular computer program, license, or
machine required for or valuable to your position. The key here is to include
things that show your qualification for and your ability to perform your job.
List supplemental courses, conferences, etc… which common applicants may
not have attended. This shows drive and determination to excel and provide
value to your employer.

About Education Dates – Again if you are concerned about
age discrimination, it may be useful to not list your graduation dates. They
are certainly not a requirement, and can cause older candidates to be discriminated against.

Should you include a photograph? – Many people are beginning to
put photographs of themselves on their resume. I generally advise against
doing this as it can be a tool which is used to discriminate against you do to
age, race, etc… However a professional headshot included with your resume
can also do wonders to separate yourself from the crowd and give your
resume a little personality. Never include a photo unless it has been taken by
a professional. Additional information on this subject is included in The Recruiter's Secret - Social Media Survival Guide

Summary – A complete and honest resume presented in the above
format will put you far ahead of your competition. I review thousands of

resumes as part of my job as a recruiter, and I can tell you that a very small percentage of the candidates I review are following this format. It's important that you do because the more you focus your resume on the value that you provide, vs. what you want the more employers will want to interview you. The average amount of time that a recruiter looks at a resume before deciding to read it fully or pass it up, is less than 10 seconds. This means that you MUST have your resume in a format that is easy for the reader to find all of the information that is important to him, and it has to do a good job of selling your value. Following the above format is your best bet to do this.

Resume Template - Below is a template to get you started on designing an effective resume. It is just a sample with generic data from a fictional candidate, but it should be useful as a guide to help you design your own. You will want to provide more complete information than what is presented here.

John Smith
123 Mystreet, Mytown, OH.
Cell: 123-456-7890
Home: 123-456-7890
Office: 123-456-7890

Career Summary (or Key Accomplishments)
I am an experienced Controller with 20 years experience in full cycle accounting. For XYZ Corp I reduced overhead by 25% in my first 6 months by reducing waste from running lights in empty rooms. For ABC Inc. I eliminated redundant overhead expenses increasing profitability by 10%.
Employment History
2001 – Present ABC Corp – Controller
Key Accomplishments:
- Reduced X by doing Y

- Managed Staff of Z
- Improved G by action W

Key Responsibilities
- Balance Books
- Weekly Meetings with CEO and CFO
- Set Departmental Budgets

1999-2001 – Temporarily Left workforce to Care for Relative

1991-1999 - XYZ Corp – Sr Accountant
Key Accomplishments:
- Reduced X by doing Y
- Managed Staff of Z
- Improved G by action W

Key Responsibilities
- Balance Books
- Weekly Meetings with Controller
- Set Departmental Budgets

Key Qualifications (or Technologies)
Microsoft Word, Microsoft Excel, Powerpoint, Microsoft Access, Quickbooks, SAP, Sage, Peoplesoft, ADP Online Payroll.
Certifications
CPA, MBA, CFA, CFP,
Education
XYZ State University – 1995 – MBA Accounting,
ABC College – 1989 – Bachelor Finance.

13

PREPARE A MARKETING SUMMARY

The information for this can be pulled directly off of your resume and it is basically a combination of all of the highlights of your resume. This is possibly the most important document that you will be preparing so take your time and get this right.

- It IS NOT a cover letter (Which lists your goals, etc.... and is generic)

- It IS NOT a Resume (Which is a complete picture of your education and career)

- It IS a one page brochure of your VALUE from an employer's prospective.

- Your Most Valuable accomplishments (Quantifiable)

- Key Responsibilities etc... that provide value to the employer.

- List a one sentence highlight of your 5 most positive references

This is your chance to "Sell Yourself" a little. Because it's not a resume, you won't be constrained by the reverse chronological format of a traditional resume. You can list accomplishments from multiple employers all in one section. You can also use the summary to present a short story of how you overcame an obstacle for your previous employer, etc...

Remember that this needs to be short and sweet, and full of value to the employer. It differs from a cover letter in that it is not going to have an objective, is not going to mention anything you want, but is only used to give an "executive overview" of what you bring to the table, the results you have achieved, and the references that will back that up.

Here is an example of a Marketing Page It goes just over two pages due to the large list of accomplishments and references supplied for this particular candidate. You'll notice that I have actually highlighted and bolded many things on this document. I don't recommend doing this for a marketing page that is being sent physically. I used this particular document as a follow up e-mail to leads generated over the phone. You will also be able to put in identifiable contact information. As a recruiter we have to keep our candidates identities private, so identifiable information such as the candidate's name and employer's company names, are removed. You will most likely want to include those details in your marketing summary, however you may wish to keep your current employer's identity private if you are conducting a confidential job search.

Highlights

• Experienced in complex Software / Services sales with single sales of up to $36 Million

• Insurance Industry Infrastructure Software Company: Improved services revenue over 200% in first year.

• Infrastructure Change Management Software & Consulting: Improved quarterly services revenue 400%

• Top ERP Software & Services Company: Improved annual services revenue over 90% on sales of over $20Million

• Internationally Known Consulting and Implementation Services Company: Improved net operating margin by 75% on $20-30Million annual services sales.

• Nationally Known Midwest IT Consulting Company: As an active partner grew company from 20 to approx 300 employees resulting in the company eventually being acquired by international consulting firm, and later becoming the IT consulting division of a big 6 accounting / consulting company.

This candidate is an experienced leader, motivator, and customer service professional.

• He is experienced in the sales and implementation of leading ERP software to large publicly traded companies, and midsized private companies alike.

• Routinely Closes Sales to VP and "C Level" executives from major brands like: Levi Strauss, Advanced Micro Devices, Microsoft, Nestle, Nike, Starbucks, Polo / Ralph Lauren, National City Bank, Walt Disney, etc…

• Experienced in Building Sales / Services divisions for Global Top 10 Software / Consulting Companies – Recruiting staff, Training / Motivation, Key Account Management, Problem Account Turnaround.

• Proven manager of staff of over (200+) Sales and Consulting Staff across Multiple Continents.

- Proven Manager of Multi Million Dollar Departmental Budgets.
- Has demonstrated ability to reduce receivables, increase sales, and boost profitability.
- Consistently improves billing utilization of staff to reduce wasted "Bench Time"

References:

In the process of doing my diligence on this candidate I have interviewed dozens of former supervisors, peers, subordinates and customers. Every single person that I have identified as a contact (Not just candidate supplied references) has given a positive review. On the following pages are samples of the feedback I have received.

Reference Letter Excerpts:

…I was so pleased with xxxxxxxx's performance at the first company, that I hired xxxxxx again at a subsequent company… … managed a staff of Project Managers and Consultants performing full functioned ERP software implementations… …to "turn-around" a cadre of unhappy customers, to the point of having them order additional software and services…

…an efficient and effective manager and he had his eye on the satisfaction of our prospects and customers…

…extremely organized, developed individual business plans for accounts…

…I would hire/work with Xxxxx in any professional services position/organization. His involvement would be an asset second to none…

… was committed and excelled at business development and management within the company. Our company was very successful in large part due to the efforts of xxxxxx….

… ran the professional services division in North America…did an excellent job building out our group and bringing it to profitability. As his former supervisor, I definitely would hire xxxxx again…

…was a great teacher and his experience in dealing with clients, understanding their issues and formulating solutions was invaluable to me as I was learning about the consulting business…

…is articulate, credible and targets the customers' value points while maintaining his post-sale attention to project performance…

… is an engaging professional that comes to the table prepared and more than ready to work hard…

… is able to turn a disaster implementation into a happy referenceable customer…

… provided a professional presence that gave me a chance to become the professional that I am today.

…He was wonderful at dealing with clients, in both sales and support roles…

… managed several profit centers and was co-manager of a consulting organization of over 200 professional consultants and subordinate managers… …helped lead the company through a period of rapid growth… …also took great pride in helping new consultants learn their profession…

14

THE RECRUITER'S SECRET TO TURBO CHARGING YOUR REFERENCES

The following is a reprint of the Recruiter's Secret to Turbo Charging Your References

The Recruiter's Secret to Turbo Charging your References

One of the most valuable tools you can have when searching for a job is quality references. Just like testimonials or product reviews on Amazon.com, Bestbuy.com, Walmart.com, etc... References give a 3rd party opinion on your past performance and character. This gives the person evaluating your resume quality information about you that they really want to know, and that most candidates aren't providing. Having quality references prior to submitting a resume or application can move you from the middle of the pack right to the front.

How many references should I provide?

Most candidates provide 3 names and phone numbers when asked for references. Sometimes they include them on their resume, and sometimes only provide them after they have been requested by their prospective employer. This provides the proactive jobseeker a tremendous opportunity. I recommend submitting as many pre-written references as possible. When I'm actively marketing a candidate to employers I'll sometimes have as many as twenty written references from past supervisors, co-workers, employees, customers, etc... Putting in this work really shows an employer that you are well liked, and trusted by people that know you professionally.

Who should I ask for references?

I recommend asking anyone that is in a position to objectively comment on your value to your employer. Valuable references can come from Supervisors, Co-workers (Particularly if they have moved on to prestigious positions within other companies), direct reports (Particularly if they have moved on to prestigious positions within other companies), and Customers with whom you've had direct relationship. If you have direct contact with customers, a customer's recommendation can show that you are a valuable asset to your employer. I don't recommend using too many "Personal" references, or people that you are friends with but have not worked with. They are suspect to employers and don't provide information about you as an employee.

What is the best way to go about getting references to submit to your targeted employer?

The best way to get references to send is simply to ask. You'll be surprised how many people are glad to give you a reference if you just ask. I recommend giving them a template to follow, but insist that they answer in their own words. IE Send them a letter or e-mail with several questions regarding your performance, and ask them to answer the questions. You might need to spend a little time explaining what you are looking for, but most people are generous and like to help.

What about social networking sites like LinkedIn?

I don't recommend using social networking sites like LinkedIn to gather references. Many people openly solicit or "trade" recommendations on that site so recommendations posted there may be suspect to an employer. That being said, references can be taken from LinkedIn if they are legitimate, and you include contact information for the reference in addition to the LinkedIn information.

Always include contact information

You should always include full contact information on all references that you use including Phone Number, Current Company and Title. I also recommend including information such as what the person's relationship was at the time you worked together. This full disclosure gives the employer confidence in the accuracy and honesty of the references, as well as the opportunity to verify the information by calling the reference personally. If possible get the references directly on company letterhead from the reference's company. This is an additional assurance that the reference is real and trustworthy.

Side Benefits

You might be surprised to find that the process of asking for references can actually land you a job. Asking your network of colleagues and former co-workers to think about and express what a wonderful employee you were lets your existing network know that you are on the market. I've seen many cases where this has resulted in interviews and even job offers right on the spot.

Risks

If you are currently employed, you MUST make sure that you are only asking for references from people that you can trust not to blow the whistle on your job search activities and risk your current employment. This means that you probably can't ask current supervisors and co-workers for references, so you'll want to concentrate on really reaching out to your network that you built at former employers. This is the one place where LinkedIn is very valuable because it is a way for you to solicit written recommendations from your current co-workers employer's and customers without raising any red flags that it is for purposes of a career search. You are just building your profile, and using to benefit your company.

Summary

Building a portfolio of references is one of the easiest things you can do to truly TURBO CHARGE your career search. Being the one candidate with a resume that also includes 5 or 10 pages of written recommendations will do more than you can possibly imagine towards moving you directly to the front of the pack, and getting you the interview. Then it's up to you

15

PREPARE A MARKETING PACKAGE

OK, if you are still with me, by now you've
* ❖ Decided to explore your options
* ❖ Determined the cost of being unemployed or underemployed
* ❖ Researched your job market
* ❖ Researched target companies
* ❖ Identified key employees at your target companies
* ❖ Prepared your resume – including quantifiable achievements, and skills
* ❖ Started collecting references
* ❖ Wondered, "When do I start marketing myself?"

Well, now would be the time to start. In the traditional job-seeker approach that all of your competition is using, the way to market yourself is to pick up the paper and send identical copies of your resume to any ads that match your qualifications, then go online to the job boards and do the same. You aren't going to do that though, because you know that:

- ❖ The average jobseeker can send up to 100 applications for each call they receive from an employer.
- ❖ It takes up to 5 calls to land a face to face interview
- ❖ It takes up to 5 face to face interviews to land a job
- ❖ That's a total of 500 applications sent out before you land the job you are looking for
- ❖ An average of 6 months to 1 yr to land a same level to better level position

These numbers are largely because the average jobseeker is stuck in the middle of the herd of zebras. To the hiring company they all look alike: They've all sent resume's all are reasonably qualified, and have all followed the same procedure. One of them might get snapped up, but because of the large numbers they all have a small chance.

To illustrate this point consider the following

- ❖ If there are 100 people competing for the same prize, each has exactly a 1% chance of winning and a 99% chance of losing.
- ❖ If there are 50 people competing for the same prize, each has exactly a 2% chance of winning and a 98% chance of losing.
- ❖ If there are 25 people competing for the same prize, each has exactly a 4% chance of winning and a 96% chance of losing.
- ❖ If there are 10 people competing for the same prize, each has exactly a 10% chance of winning and a 90% chance of losing.
- ❖ If there are 5 people competing for the same prize, each has exactly a 20% chance of winning and an 80% chance of losing.
- ❖ If there are 2 people competing for the same prize, each has exactly a 50% chance of winning and a 50% chance of losing.
- ❖ If there are 1 person competing for a prize, he has exactly a 100% chance of winning and a 0% chance of losing.

The example above is a little simplistic because it assumes that every person competing will have the exact same chance, which is of course not quite true. Every person will have a different chance depending on their skills, experience, background, likeability, professionalism, etc... but when YOU submit YOUR resume you have no idea where you fit in with the rest of the group. So statistically speaking you have just as good a chance at being the front runner as you do being at the bottom of the list.

Once you've started interviewing you are sure that your odds are pretty good right? Usually a company will interview at least 10 people by phone or in person for the first round on any given position. 10% chance of success, 90% chance of losing. Well you made it past the first round, you had better start packing right? They may interview 5 of those same people in the second round – 20% chance of winning 80% chance of losing. You made it past that round and have been informed that you are a finalist, time to draft the resignation letter now right? They'll then usually interview 3 finalists – 33% chance of winning 66% chance of losing. As you can see when taking the traditional jobseeker approach your odds are always stacked against you and in the company's favor.

It also assumes that a company will definitely hire one of the applicants which is of course not always the case. I've known of cases where a company screened, hundreds of applicants, interviewed dozens, and got down to 2 or 3 finalists. Then decided that none of the candidates were good enough and started the hunt over. I've seen many times where a company has cancelled the job order at some time during the hiring process. So your chances of beating the competition on any given job are actually significantly lower than what is illustrated above. This is why it can take as many as 100 applications to generate a single phone interview.

I know you are thinking that if I have a 1% chance of winning on 1 job, if I just apply to 100 jobs that will give me a 100% chance of winning. Well, I'm sorry to be the one to tell you this, but that's not how it works.

Traditional Jobseeker Odds
❖ Submit your application to 100 job openings
❖ 100 other candidates submit to each opening
❖ This means you have a 100 / 10,000 chance of getting an interview. (100 applications are your's out of a total of 10,000 total applications)
❖ So instead of increasing your odds to 100%, you have kept your odds at exactly 1% on any of the jobs that you have applied to.

Again this is a simplistic example and it doesn't factor in all of the intangibles, like skills, experience, etc… but is does illustrate the point that if you follow the same path that everyone else is following your odds of landing an equivalent or better job compared to your current or last one are always going to be slim.

Now you're thinking, WOW, it must be impossible to get a job. Not really! You have to be aware of the math involved so that you understand the significance of your marketing package. The effective execution of your marketing package is what will set you apart from the other 99 applicants competing for YOUR prize. Remember that the other 99 applicants have sent a generic, or even a mildly customized resume, and that they are hoping to beat those same odds. If you build my marketing package and follow my marketing plan you will be the ONLY person considered for a job at many of the companies that you interview with. This doesn't mean you have a 100% chance of being hired, your interviewing skills will have a lot to do with that, but you've definitely got to believe that your odds are better than doing it the traditional way.

What's in the marketing package?

I recommend sending a marketing package because it separates you from all of the other applicants that a company sees that send only a resume and a cover letter. This makes you look like a professional and someone that the company NEEDS to look at, not just some random person looking for a job. This gives the impression that the company needs you more than you need them. This increases your value because you will be sought after.

I prepare marketing packages for many of the candidates that I market to employers. This is particularly effective in the executive ranks, but I've seen it practiced by recruiters that are marketing production workers, clerical workers, accountants, lawyers, nurses, middle management, machinists, laborers, contractors, engineers, and pretty much any position you can think of.

The marketing package for every candidate will be different. Yours will be different from any that I've ever used for any of my clients. When designing your marketing package think for a while about the last time you looked at a new car, or a new printer for your computer, etc… When you look at a car and test drive it the dealer will probably give you some brochures with glossy photos, key specifications customer testimonials, etc… (You can walk into any car dealer and they'll gladly give you handfuls of these just for asking). These marketing brochures or binders with their flashy ads and attractive layouts give the car an appearance of exclusivity, quality, and gives examples of how it will not only meet your needs but provide value in ways you may not have considered previously.

Car companies spend large amounts of time and money developing these brochures because they know that when you purchase a car it will be a major investment that you will have to pay for and live with for years. Most people feel that their car is an important part of their image, and a reflection of who they are. You won't take the decision lightly and giving you an attractive brochure helps you make your decision and reinforces it after the sale. When a company hires you, it will be a major decision that they will have to pay for and live with for years. Much like a car to a driver, employees are the face of the company and a reflection on the management.

I'm not saying that you should produce a marketing package for yourself that rivals a brochure for a Lexus, but I do think it's important that you understand that you should put some thought and care into the materials used in and the presentation of your marketing package.

What will the marketing package include?
❖ Binder, Report Cover or Folder from an office supply house – The higher the quality the better. You don't have to go crazy here, but don't buy the cheapest thing either. A good quality binder or report cover will only cost a couple of dollars each, and it is the first impression of you that the employer will get. You never get a second chance at a first impression, so extra money spent here can be an excellent investment. If cost is an issue with the volume that you will be sending then send less expensive binders to lower priority targets. IE HR departments can get less expensive binders, while CEO's get the top of the line.

- ❖ A label for the folder – Depending on your binder or folder there may be space for a label. I recommend purchasing large labels at least 4 X 6 or 5 X 7 to place here. Include your name and a one line description of yourself, and optionally a photo. If you have a report cover that has room for a full sheet of paper, you can always design a nice cover page and use that instead of a label.
- ❖ A One Page Marketing Summary – Inside the folder the first thing that should be seen is your one page marketing summary. The information for this can be pulled directly off of your resume and it is basically a combination of all of the highlights of your resume. This was covered in detail earlier in this program, but here is a summary to refresh your memory. Please remember to customize this for each employer you target.
- ❖ It IS NOT a cover letter (Which lists your goals, etc.... and is generic)
- ❖ It IS NOT a Resume (Which is a complete picture of your education and career)
- ❖ It IS a one page brochure of your VALUE from an employer's prospective.
- ❖ Your Most Valuable accomplishments (Quantifiable)
- ❖ Key Responsibilities etc… that provide value to the employer.
- ❖ List a one sentence highlight of your 5 most positive references
- ❖ Examples of your work (Portfolio) If appropriate – Including examples or photos of things you have designed, built, patents you have been awarded, or other such accomplishments as a separate section is an excellent idea that will really set you apart from the competition. Showing

what you can do is significantly more effective than telling someone what you can do.

- ❖ Newspaper articles, interviews, or other published works – If you have been interviewed, published, or otherwise noted by a respected third party, including copies is an excellent idea.

- ❖ Your Resume – The complete resume with quantifiable accomplishments, and focused on value provided to your employers – We went into detail on resume preparation earlier in the program.

- ❖ Printed versions of all of your recommendations

- ❖ One recommendation letter Maximum per page (If a letter is two pages, use two sheets of paper, if it's two sentences, still use one sheet for that letter.)

- ❖ A CD with digital copies of your documents – Because most companies now operate in a digital age, including electronic copies of all of the documents in your marketing package in MS word And or PDF format will help the company distribute it through the right channels once you have gotten in the door. It allow them to print multiple copies and again, it will set you apart because none of your competition is doing this.

A note about quality

When choosing paper to print your resume, marketing page, and references on make sure to use a high quality white paper with a heavy weight. I don't think it's necessary to use cardstock, glossy photo paper, etc… for your resume but don't use the cheapest copy paper either. You want your marketing package to present you in a quality light, and using poor quality materials sends the opposite message. I also don't recommend using the "Resume Paper" found in a typical office supply store. It is a relic of a time when resumes were typed out one at a time on a typewriter and stored in paper files.

Resume paper was a way to make your resume stand out from the normal typing paper that all of the other resumes that an employer had in their paper files was printed on. Today however your paper resume will probably be scanned and converted to a word document or PDF and stored in an applicant tracking system So having a resume printed on a quality white paper makes that easier and will be appreciated.

A note about photos.

It's becoming more common to include a photo in a resume (This includes social networking sites like Facebook and LinkedIn that approximate a resume) lately. I am often asked if this is a good idea. To be honest I have mixed feelings about it, because if you have a really good photo and are really good looking it will probably give you an advantage over other jobseekers. Including a photo in your resume also illustrates the fact that you are a person, and not a piece of paper, a living breathing human that the reader can identify with and connect to. However, a photo can also be damaging to your chances of landing a job for many reasons, and can be used as a tool to discriminate against a jobseeker. So I'll leave it up to you on whether you should include it, but I will provide some guidelines on how to use them.

If you use a photograph make sure that it's a professional looking headshot and has been retouched by a photographer. It isn't that expensive to have a professional headshot taken and retouched, but the advantage of having a photo that is looks totally professional and that could be used in a magazine is significant. This type of photo will make you look more professional and more attractive and is the same type of photo used every day by real estate agents, recruiters, TV news anchors, and Actors. There is real value to be gained from presenting yourself this way.

On the other hand, NEVER use a photo that looks amateurish. A photo of yourself standing against a wall looking like you are about to be booked, or a webcam photo with a cluttered background will significantly diminish any perception of value that you have worked so hard to present. NEVER use a photo that shows you engaged in a hobby like hiking, walking your dog, biking, etc... I know it sounds obvious, but you would be surprised how many people present themselves online and on their resume's using photos that are hastily taken and not very well thought out. It's not unusual to find a jobseeker has posted photos of himself online engaging in embarrassing or illegal activity. So my advice here is take serious thought about what you include in your marketing package or online.

❖ Don't use photo if you think it can cause you to be discriminated against. Discrimination while illegal, and immoral, still happens. Your photo can cause you to be discriminated against based on your Age, Race, Religion, Hobbies, etc.... So be aware of this when you decide to include a photo in your resume or online profiles.

"Wait, this looks like it will cost me money, and I'm out of work and money is tight!!!"

I understand what you are thinking here. But the truth is you are wrong. While you will have to spend some money on supplies and postage the truth is that this is actually saving you a lot of money. Let's be very conservative here and assume that following my plan will only get you a job two weeks faster than you could have gotten one on your own (in reality you'll save months). Then let's go wild and say you spend $500 on supplies, postage, and other misc costs to follow this plan. Now let's say you are unemployed and formerly made $35,000 a year. We've already established that it costs you $845 for each and every week that you remain unemployed. That means that for the two weeks extra that it takes you to find a job it costs you $1,690. If it costs you $500 to follow this plan, you have saved $1190. Even Warren Buffet would love the return on that investment. And there will most likely be a significant difference in your compensation at your new job if you follow this plan vs. if you don't. Now do that math with what you actually made, and see how much you'll save.

16

LET'S START HUNTING

Take your list of companies and send your marketing package to them in a quality envelope. The envelope should be large enough to include the Don't be afraid to include a free gift to make your package lumpy. If you do this the gift must be relevant to your marketing package. IE send a Key, and a card that says I'll be your Key employee, or Send a baseball and say "Hiring me is a Home Run" (Please don't copy this exactly it's a bit cheesy) Including something in the envelope, or even just using Fedex, UPS, or Priority Mail will increase the chances of your envelope being opened. Additionally if you use these services you can get a delivery confirmation so you'll know immediately when your package has been delivered.

Who should you send your marketing package to?

OK, now you have your marketing package together, who should you send it to? We have to send it to someone that can make a decision on actually hiring you.

Hiring roles within a company

In small Mom & Pop companies there really isn't any segmentation of a hiring role vs. every other role. So naturally the owner will be the person to speak to most of the time. But as we look at larger companies they will have specialized HR departments and internal recruiters who's job it is to "screen out" unwanted candidates, and recruit or attract desirable ones. The problem for you is that these people don't generally have the final say over who gets hired by the company. They get a request from someone in the management chain to find someone that fits a certain profile, and then they create a job description and go about the business of finding someone to fill that role. They place ads online and in the papers, and screen applicants in their computers and over the phone. The lucky ones get passed on to a department manager (your eventual supervisor) and then the SR. management. This is where you get into competition with large numbers of other applicants and your chances go down.

Your goal is to rise above the noise and become the ONLY candidate under consideration. You'll do that by identifying the decision makers that are actually able to make a decision on hiring you, and get to them before you have to start the cycle from the beginning and become 1 out of 100.

We are going to use the tools presented previously like Hoovers, Manta, Zoominfo, LinkedIn, and especially Jigsaw to identify the key decision makers within the company that you will send your marketing package to. The positions you will target will depend on what your target position is within the company. For example, if you are a machinist, you'll want to target a shop forman, a production manager, etc… If you are a salesman target the Sales manager, VP of Sales, CEO, etc… Target any titles that you know will be your direct supervisor. Then also target HIS supervisor. It's OK to send your marketing package to more than one person within the company. I typically will send a package to several people within the company because you never know who'll see it and identify a need within the company for someone just like you.

❖ Key executives
  o Owner
  o CEO
  o COO
  o President
  o Founder
❖ Potential supervisors
  o CIO
  o CFO
  o VP level in your department
  o Manager Level in your department
  o Also send to Human Resources (HR)

You will typically be able to identify at least 3 or 4 targets within a company to send your package to. You don't want to waste time or money sending it to everyone in the company, but take some time and use the research tools I gave you to figure out who makes sense in your specific case. There is really no limit to how many people you can send it to, and you can always send a cheaper version to some people and the full blown package to your key targets.

How many companies should you target?

I recommend targeting 10 to 20 employers at a time. And send to at least 3 contacts within each company that you target. This will represent a total of 30-60 marketing packages sent. If you have followed my instructions and put together a professional looking presentation, and targeted your companies well, this should result in at least one serious interview and possibly more. These are not the HR department screening you out, only 4 more rounds to go type of interviews, I'm talking about you are already to the final round and if you ace this you are hired kind of interviews. Remember that nobody else is doing this, and you WILL stand out from the crowd by doing it. This makes you look serious, and unique. You will be in a stronger position than the average jobseeker because you will already have created interest in yourself from the higher ups in the company.

Repeat this process weekly until you have an offer that you want to accept. Don't get frustrated by not getting hired the first week you try this. If you send to 10 targeted companies a week, that's 40 per month, and 520 in a year.

And again remember this is significantly different than applying to 10 or 20 jobs online per week. When you apply online, your resume goes into the computer, it's graded, and then it might get looked at by someone in HR who might call you, and who might pass your resume on along with 10 others to the next round of interviews. Sending out marketing packages to multiple people in 10 companies will get your resume in front of decision makers by yourself with no competition. How many jobs would you have to apply to online and

78

phone interviews would you have to go through to get the same re-sults?

The more companies you send to each week the better your chances are of getting interviews. However, don't skip the step of doing research on each company you send to. Demonstrating that you know something about them is just as important as getting noticed in the first place. It is very easy to fall into the trap of sending out a sin-gle package for every company. Take the time to customize your package for each employer or job that you are targeting. Make sure that your resume and marketing page are relevant to the needs of your target employer. This will increase the number of calls you get after send out your package.

17

FOLLOWING UP

When you apply to a job online there is generally not even a confirmation sent to you that they got your resume and you'll have no idea if anyone has ever even read it. You won't know the names of the people that are looking; you will be completely at their mercy.

When you follow my program you will know who has received your package and when. Remember we sent them with a delivery confirmation via Fedex, UPS, or Priority Mail. When some-one receives a priority package with a free gift inside, it doesn't go in the regular junk mail pile, it gets opened and looked at. So if you don't get a call from anyone that you sent your package to, follow up a day or two after the got your package with a phone call. When the receptionist or admin assistant asks "Is he expecting your call?" you can honestly answer "Yes he is!" Don't call and expect to be hired on the spot, just call and offer to clarify any points on your resume that they have questions on. And if you get an answer stating that they aren't hiring, not interested at this time, etc... don't get discouraged, because one of the companies you send it to will be interested. Don't excessively hound any of the companies you have targeted, and ho-nestly don't expect anything from any of them in particular. You are marketing yourself as a hot commodity, and the key is to put your package in front of as many relevant decision makers as possible.

When you do get a call from one of the companies you tar-geted, don't be surprised. You'll probably hear things like:

- "Nobody has ever approached us in this way"
- "Nobody has ever shown this kind of initiative"
- "Nobody has ever shown us that they understand our business this way"
- "I'm flattered that someone like you would be inter-ested in working for us"

Remember though you STILL have to go through your inter-view, and negotiate your salary. But at this point you have set yourself apart from the competition, you have represented yourself as a star, and you have secured the respect of someone that you'd like to work for. The interview should be a piece of cake.

Congratulations and good luck.

ADDITIONAL RESOURCES

We have a lot of additional resources available to you at www.TheRecruitersSecret.com

On our website we have training videos with additional and more detailed information for many of the techniques outlined in this book, as well as a downloadable PDF and MP3 version of this book so that you can take it with you and listen on the go.

We also have several services available to help you market yourself effectively:

- ❖ Resume Review
- ❖ Marketing Profile Assistance
- ❖ Reference Check Assistance
- ❖ Networking Assistance
- ❖ Social Media Profile Review and Optimization Services
- ❖ Dedicated Candidate Marketing Services (Only for Qualified Candidates)

Since you have purchased the paperback version of this book you will be entitled to a discount on the website membership.

Go to www.TheRecruitersSecret.com and request a coupon.

ABOUT THE AUTHOR

John Kaufman is currently President of Nexmation, LLC. a national Recruiting Agency headquartered in Cleveland, OH.

He has been involved in consulting recruiting and staffing since the late 1990's. His start in IT consulting came during the rush to ready systems for Y2K, when he used his extensive network of contacts to provide Recruiting & Staffing services for other consulting companies that couldn't locate contractors to work on large scale complex projects. Later his first IT consulting company transformed into a nationally known web hosting company that maintained 100% compounded annual sales growth for 10 years before being sold to private investors.

John recruited, hired, managed, and fired IT executives, salesmen, customer service specialists, and technical personnel like developers, and networking specialist that worked to maintain his company's growth. This gives him a unique insight into what works and what doesn't in a job search. He knows what gets a successful employer's attention and what doesn't.

John is a nationally recognized recruiting expert, quoted by Smart Money, Harvard Kennedy School, Cincinnati Enquirer, and others.

www.ingramcontent.com/pod-product-compliance
Lightning Source LLC
Chambersburg PA
CBHW071243170526
45165CB00003B/1213